Two Dollar Radio

Guide to

VEGAN
COOKING

THE PINK EDITION

*Recipes, Stories Behind the Recipes,
and Inspiration for Vegan Cheffing.*

Two Dollar Radio
Books too loud to Ignore

WHO WE ARE TWO DOLLAR RADIO is a family-run outfit dedicated to reaffirming the cultural and artistic spirit of the publishing industry. We aim to do this by presenting bold works of literary merit, each book, individually and collectively, providing a sonic progression that we believe to be too loud to ignore.

TwoDollarRadio.com

Proudly based in

Columbus
OHIO

@TwoDollarRadio

@TwoDollarRadio

/TwoDollarRadio

ALL PHOTOS, ART, RECIPES, AND TEXT→
Eric Obenauf

Page 111: Photo by Sandi Benedicta on Unsplash (https://unsplash.com/photos/b7F8mxFgAMY)

Two Dollar Radio
HEADQUARTERS

The exterior of Two Dollar Radio Headquarters, circa 2019.

COME VISIT US IN CENTRAL OHIO!

Two Dollar Radio Headquarters is a bar, café, plant-based watering hole, and bookstore specializing in the best in independently published literature.

TwoDollarRadioHQ.com

@TwoDollarRadioHQ

@TwoDollarHQ

/TwoDollarRadioHQ

Converting to Metrics

VOLUME MEASUREMENT CONVERSIONS

U.S.	METRIC
¼ teaspoon	1.25 ml
½ teaspoon	2.5 ml
¾ teaspoon	3.75 ml
1 teaspoon	5 ml
1 tablespoon	15 ml
¼ cup	62.5 ml
½ cup	125 ml
¾ cup	187.5 ml
1 cup	250 ml

WEIGHT MEASUREMENT CONVERSIONS

U.S.	METRIC
1 ounce	28.4 g
8 ounces	227.5 g
16 ounces (1 pound)	455 g

COOKING TEMPERATURE CONVERSIONS

To convert temperatures in Fahrenheit to Celsius, subtract 32 and multiply by .5556 (or $\frac{5}{9}$): $\mathbf{C = (°F - 32) \times \frac{5}{9}}$

EXAMPLE: $(350°F - 32) \times \frac{5}{9} = 176.667°C$

HYPERBOLIC

TABLE OF CONTENTS

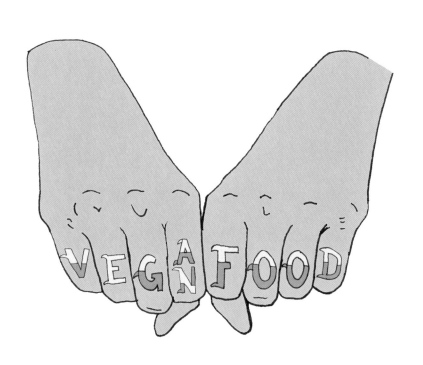

Editor's Note About Accessibility of the Recipes

The editors would like to acknowledge that not everyone has an industrial kitchen at their disposal with exotic spices and rare ingredients. We don't either! The goal with the recipes presented in the *Two Dollar Radio Guide to Vegan Cooking* series is to make them accessible for cheffing in a home kitchen.

"No one asked Gene Kelly
'Why do you dance?'"

—TOM CRUISE
(WHEN ASKED WHY HE PERFORMS
HIS OWN STUNTS IN FILMS.)

Why We Dance

A common lament by those looking to make the jump to a vegan diet is a reluctance to give things up. "I could never give up tuna noodle casserole," they say. Never mind it's canned tuna and noodles lathered in mayonnaise, nary a vegetable in sight; food blanched white, otherwise known as a Midwestern heart attack in meal form.

The prospect of giving up cheese, for us, was like the prospect of walking on our hands; we didn't want to just voluntarily do it. Which is why the first challenge we set for ourselves—our Mount Everest, so to speak—was to craft dairy-free cheeses. After a seared eyebrow, more than one sleepless night, a blender upgrade, and a bruised trachea resulting from a hot-yoga mishap, thus was born *cheeze* with a "z."

So we ask you: what if you didn't have to really sacrifice anything from your diet? What if you could have cheeze that tastes so good magical fairies dance around your blender with wands that they wave around and stuff? That's why we dance.

—Jean-Claude van Randy and Speed Dog

Type-written on a Stenograph Stentura 8000LX.
Franklin County Courthouse, Columbus, Ohio, May 24, 2022.
Let it be entered into the record.

CHEEZE IS
THE BEST!

CHEEZE

**Pimento Cheeze
is a new animal.**

Cream Cheeze,
pictured here on a Taco

CREAM CHEEZE

THE DISH: Cream cheeze is just a good thing to keep stocked in the fridge. One of our favorite snacks in the history of snacks are crackers with cream cheeze and spicy jam. Cream cheeze is also a great fatty addition to sandwiches and toasted bagels. If you'd like to make a more firm cream cheeze, simply withhold the hot water from the below recipe.

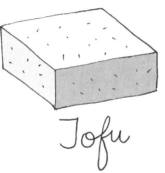

Tofu

RECIPE

1 cup cashews (soaked)
4 ounces firm tofu
¼ cup hot water
2 tablespoons nutritional yeast
1 tablespoon lemon juice
1 tablespoon apple cider vinegar
1 teaspoon salt
1 piece garlic

CHEFFING INSTRUCTIONS

- Soak the cashews in hot water for at least 15 minutes.
- Add ingredients to a blender and blend until smooth.

PAIRING SUGGESTIONS

Did you see the note above about putting cream cheeze on crackers with spicy jam? It also goes great with carrot lox or on a classy bagel (see Jalapeño Popper Bagels—p. 91).

FOUNTAIN OF YOUTH PIMENTO CHEEZE SPREAD

THE DISH: This vegan cheeze spread has notes of North Florida sunshine embedded in it. Extra credit if you soak your cashews in water from Ponce de Leon's "Fountain of Youth" in St. Augustine, Florida. Believe me when I say you haven't felt this buoyant since Uncle Gary let you ride along to Publix on family vacation.

RECIPE

1 cup cashews (soaked)
1 cup vegan mayonnaise (p. 107)
½ cup nutritional yeast
¼ cup diced pimentos (jarred)
1 tablespoon smoked paprika
Salt + pepper to taste

CHEFFING INSTRUCTIONS

- Soak the cashews in hot water for at least 15 minutes.
- Add ingredients (save half the pimentos) to a blender and blend until smooth.
- Transfer to dish. Add remaining pimentos and stir into mixture.

PAIRING SUGGESTIONS

Sunscreen or body oil (must be coconut fragrance).
Sandra Bullock movies.
Dancing awkwardly cause you're wearing flip-flops.

Pimento Cheeze Spread

Sliceable Mozzarella Cheeze

SLICEABLE MOZZARELLA CHEEZE

THE DISH: This cheeze can be grated on pizzas, sliced on sandwiches or for fancy cheeze plates, and will even melt when heated.

RECIPE

3 cups hot water
1 cup cashews (soaked)
½ cup refined coconut oil
½ cup tapioca flour
3 tablespoons nutritional yeast
3 tablespoons kappa carrageenan
2 tablespoons lemon juice
1 tablespoon apple cider vinegar
2 teaspoons salt
1 to 2 teaspoons liquid smoke
1 teaspoon white miso paste
½ teaspoon onion powder
2 pieces garlic

CHEFFING INSTRUCTIONS

• Soak the cashews in hot water for at least 15 minutes.
• Add all ingredients (hot water last) to a blender and blend thoroughly.
• The mixture will thicken along the outside of the blender. When you notice air bubbles rise in the center and it appears smooth, it's blended.
• Quickly transfer to a lidded container that will be easy to remove cheeze block from, and refrigerate.

BUFFALO QUESO

THE DISH: You can, and should, put this buffalo queso on everything you want to eat. It's like Batman's utility belt, but vegan.

RECIPE

4 ounces firm tofu
1 cup cashews (soaked)
1 cup nutritional yeast
¾ cup non-sweetened plant milk (oat, soy, nut, rice...)
¾ cup vegan buffalo sauce of your choice
⅓ cup oil
1½ tablespoons smoked paprika
½ head of garlic
Salt + pepper to taste

CHEFFING INSTRUCTIONS

• Soak the cashews in hot water for at least 15 minutes.
• Add ingredients to a blender and blend until smooth.
• Garnish with coconut bacon (p. 47) or scallions.

PAIRING SUGGESTIONS

A helmet, cause you'll feel immortal after eating this.
Toss buffalo queso with noodles for Mac & Cheeze.
Put on tacos, use as a dip for chips… Just always keep some handy in your fridge to ward off Hunger Demons.

Mac & Cheeze made with
Buffalo Queso

Prologue: The Crystal Forest

Morning rises over the annual Gathering of the Juggalos at the Crystal Forest in northeast Ohio. Canvas tents, teepees, and makeshift shelters cover the trodden ground in a clearing in the woods. The whole scene looks hungover: there are empty spray paint canisters and 2-liter Mountain Dew bottles; a parked helicopter with a pilot slumbering in the cockpit. A shirtless man with his hair knotted in braids, clown face paint, and a rotund belly lies passed out face-up in a pickup truck bed.

A 1988 Aerostar minivan slowly drives the dirt roadway through the gathering, down the midway, past stationary rides and games, till stopping amidst a row of slumbering food stalls. The van's sliding door glides open and two figures gracefully exit and begin to expertly assemble their stall quietly so as not to wake the sleeping festival-goers.

A grill-top pings to life; a pot begins to make happy cooking sounds; two hands that sport knuckle tattoos spelling "VEGAN FOOD" (the *A* and the *N* share a knuckle) expertly chop onions and peppers.

An aroma ascends from the grill-top and is carried by the breeze: it is a quixotic scent—a conflation of multipurpose coconut oil and rock'n'roll—and it drifts over the tents, snaking its way to Bruce.

Still passed out in the truck bed, Bruce's nose twitches. His eyes jerk open and he sits upright, craning his neck from side to side in search of the source of the scent. His belly growls, hungrily. In a trance, Bruce ambles down the midway like a puppet directed by the invisible string of the quixotic scent, till he arrives at the only stall in service—the source of the aroma—where he's been summoned by the Food Gods and the Hunger Demons. Bruce peers up at the sign and furrows his brow. It proclaims "VEGAN FXXD."

The hands with the knuckle tattoos pass Bruce a monster-looking sandwich, which Bruce accepts, skeptically. *Does "vegan" mean the joy has been sucked out with a syringe?* His stomach growls angrily, propelling him into a hoagie bun that has been dipped in hot sauce and then toasted. His eyes widen as though struck by lightning. Bruce chews the sandwich, apprehensive at first, and then with vigor. It is ancient, primal, as Bruce culls a voice from the depths of his being, and shrieks into the void, "Whoop, whoop!"

The scene immediately and enthusiastically comes to life as festival-goers emerge from tents and teepees wearing face paint, their hair in eccentric braids. The midway rides buzz into action, and the helicopter blades begin to whirr. The Gathering is back on!

Randy's Uncle Gary used to say that food is a story. Well, this story is about food. More specifically, two vegan food adventurers traversing the countryside, slaying Hunger Demons.

There's Speed Dog, the drummer in the band; he keeps the beat (among his successful tours are with the Flaming Lips and Moby). He's like if Boots Riley spent his formative years in the Midwest and rode a skateboard. When Speed Dog goes to a dance and doesn't

13

sit down, he is dangerous. Speed Dog's the proud papa of a 1988 Aerostar touring van, as well as a lover of Ring Pops and animals.

And as for Speed Dog's trusted forever pal—the chef with the "VEGAN FOOD" knuckle tattoos, Jean-Claude van Randy—Randy's swagger is powered by his Kentucky Waterfall, and his Kentucky Waterfall is outstanding. Raised at Appalachian survivalist summer camps, you won't find Randy not wearing his Bagua Amulet Melong necklace.

This is the story about how Speed Dog, Randy, and a budding regional newspaper take on Karen, Karen-Katherine, the Ohio Beef Lobby, and the Central Ohio Dairy Alliance. It is not hyperbolic to say that what ensues is a conflict of epic proportions that pits millennials against boomers and hourly wage staffers against the Upper Arlington PTO. Buckle up.

Kentucky Waterfall

STARTERS

Almond Pesto &
Mozzarella Caprese—p. 17

**Almond Pesto &
Mozzarella Caprese**

ALMOND PESTO & MOZZARELLA CAPRESE

THE DISH: Look, this blasphemous almond pesto is going to give any Italian relative a heart attack. On the flip side, it has the potential to give pretty much anyone a heart attack because it captures everything you want in pesto: it's fresh, creamy, fatty, and tastes like a dream on pretty much everything. So.

TASTY AF

ALMOND PESTO RECIPE
1 cup almonds
2 cups fresh basil
1 cup fresh cilantro
1 cup oil
3 pieces garlic
1½ teaspoon salt

CHEFFING INSTRUCTIONS
• Throw it all in a blender and pulverize.
• Prove that vegan dreams do come true.

PAIRING SUGGESTIONS
Sliceable mozzarella cheeze (p. 9).
Red-checkered tablecloths.
Marty. Hey, Marty. Hey, Marty, c'mere!

CUCUMBER DILL SOUP

THE DISH: We're based in Columbus, true. But our hearts belong in warmer climates. That's why we're admirers of cold soup. (Don't @ us.)

RECIPE

2 cucumbers, seeded and diced
14 ounces firm tofu
1 cup fresh parsley
¾ cup plant milk
½ cup oil
5 tablespoons lemon juice
1 tablespoon dill
2½ teaspoons salt
1 teaspoon apple cider vinegar
1 teaspoon garlic

CHEFFING INSTRUCTIONS

- Slice cucumbers in half, length-wise. With a spoon, remove the seeds and pulpy center of cucumbers.
- Add all ingredients to a blender and pulverize.
- Serve cold.

PAIRING SUGGESTIONS

Leopard-print yoga pants.
Tiger-print yoga pants.

Cucumber Dill Soup

Lentil Soup

LENTIL SOUP

THE DISH: Cinnamon and raisins go together like beanbags and the hole in a wooden board in a cornhole game. As the raisins cook in the broth they'll re-hydrate and become plump and juicy, and bring a modest sweetness to this soup.

FAMILY-SIZE RECIPE

2 cups cooked lentils
7 cups vegetable broth
½ cup oil
½ cup raisins
1 tablespoon oregano

2 teaspoons cumin
2 teaspoons cinnamon
1 teaspoon pepper
1 carrot, sliced
½ onion, diced
5 to 6 pieces garlic

CHEFFING INSTRUCTIONS

• In a pot, simmer onion, carrot, and garlic in the oil until soft.
• Add broth, spices, cooked lentils, and raisins.
• Simmer for 30-45 minutes.
• I know what we said on the last soup recipe about liking cold soup, but definitely serve this one warm.

Hearts of Palm Ceviche

HEARTS OF PALM CEVICHE

THE DISH: We belong in warm weather. It's a recurring theme. If you've got an island somewhere to spot us or need a couple of hardcore vegan chefs, then hit us up. This hearts of palm ceviche recipe is refreshing and light.

RECIPE

14 ounces (1 jar) hearts of palm
3 roma tomatoes
¼ cup cilantro, diced
¼ cup red onion, diced
1 tablespoon lime juice
1 tablespoon jalapeño, diced
1 teaspoon coarse ground black pepper

HARDCORE
PADDLE-BOARD
SESH

CHEFFING INSTRUCTIONS

• Drain the hearts of palm jar and slice width-wise into ~1-inch circular pieces.
• In mixing bowl, add all the ingredients and mix together.

PAIRING SUGGESTIONS

A fine American lager but class it up with a lime wedge.
Board shorts and tank tops.

Kalamata Olive
Hummus

KALAMATA OLIVE HUMMUS

THE DISH: You need a go-to hummus recipe handy—we can't stress this enough. You can add it as a creamy protein-rich sauce to a wrap, or use it as a base and combine with lemon juice, lemon zest, caper juice, and capers to make a simple vegan caesar dressing.

INGREDIENTS

2 cups garbanzo beans
⅔ cup oil
¼ cup kalamata olives*
2 tablespoons lemon juice
1 tablespoon tahini
1 teaspoon cumin
½ teaspoon salt
2 pieces garlic

TASTY AF

CHEFFING INSTRUCTIONS

• Add ingredients to blender and pulverize.
• Add additional oil until hummus achieves desired consistency.

PAIRING SUGGESTIONS

Pita bread, tortilla chips, cucumbers.

Drop the olives from the recipe for a plain hummus.

Salsa Verde

SALSA VERDE

THE DISH: A solid A+ drum solo, salsa verde is the more exotic salsa. It's great to bring to a social gathering or potluck to up-stage all the clowns who brought regular salsa (yawn).

RECIPE

10 to 12 tomatillos
2 jalapeños
½ cup cilantro
¼ cup red onion, chopped
¼ cup lime juice
1 teaspoon salt
2 pieces garlic

CHEFFING INSTRUCTIONS

• Peel the husk off the tomatillos.
• In a pan, bake the tomatillos and jalapeños at 350°F until the tomatillos are soft and jalapeños blackened.
• Remove stem from jalapeños, and add all ingredients to blender.

PAIRING SUGGESTIONS

Salsa verde imparts a tart flavor to any dish.
Tacos, chips, burritos.
Extended drum solos.

GRANDMA'S SALSA

THE DISH: Fine, you caught us. We only put the salsa verde recipe first to show off and make ourselves appear more cultured. This salsa recipe is a staple. It's super quick to make and tastes light-years better than the jarred stuff at stores.

RECIPE

4 roma tomatoes
1 cup crushed tomato
¼ cup cilantro, diced
¼ cup onion, diced
1 tablespoon lime juice
1 teaspoon salt
1 teaspoon sugar
3 pieces garlic, diced
1 jalapeño, seeded and diced

CHEFFING INSTRUCTIONS

- Add roma tomatoes, crushed tomato, salt, sugar, and lime juice to blender and pulverize.
- Add diced onion, garlic, cilantro, and jalapeño and slowly blend, but don't pulverize—you want it chunky.

PAIRING SUGGESTIONS

Tacos, burritos, burgers, chips… pretty much anything!

Grandma's Salsa

Chapter 1

Columbus, Ohio, is known state-wide as the Capital City, and less broadly as the Yoga Studio of the Midwest. The arts district is cool if you're ambivalent about bros named Troy or Steve sporting Ohio State "block O" tattoos on their calves, stumbling in after a college football game and doing shots of Jäger. The Scioto River that winds through the city can be strikingly beautiful if you don't expect vistas or waves and are okay with water the color of a hangover. There are like a hundred universities that call Columbus home, which lend an open-minded, liberal arts vibe (at times). Abandoned warehouses provide an industrial aesthetic, though the manufacturing jobs left decades ago. The towns, rivers, and hills throughout Central Ohio are named after Indigenous peoples, though it's not lost on anyone that the city that dominates the region is named after the European explorer who "discovered" the country. Here, college football is king. The suburbs that ring the city are ruled by Karen and corporate chains, giving them a confrontational, Everytown vibe. All of which is to say, it's a perfect powder-keg of conflicting values and opinions cloaked beneath a Midwestern-nice veneer, ripe for two vegan rock-stars and an ambitious millennial marketing guru to make an impression.

On the South Side of town sits an unassuming two-story building. A sign that has seen better days protrudes from the brick façade of the second floor and reads "*Mid-Ohio Weekly Gazette*, owner-operated since the year Prince dropped *Purple Rain*."

On the second floor, Louise stands in her office, gazing out the window. Louise is a no-nonsense community organizer, and her office is her mirror: a strong sense of Black cultural heritage, vintage tour posters from her days as a drummer, and framed clippings from the *Gazette*. Across the street is a scraggly park, at the entrance of which is a weathered newspaper vending machine. Louise watches a man approach the vending machine before tossing an empty coffee mug into the trash bin beside it, abruptly walking on.

There's a soft knock at the door, yet Louise continues observing the newspaper vending machine. Denny, Louise's copy-editor pops his head in the room. Denny has a push-broom mustache and wears a khaki travel vest. "There's a Mr. Brett from the bank here to see you," Denny says.

A second head pops in the door frame. It's Rach, Louise's marketing guru. Rach wears black and is hip and a millennial, so she has ideas. And opinions. And she'll let you know. "His name's Brett, which completely fits him. I bet he has calf tattoos."

Louise watches as a dog-walker—with, like, ten leashes leading to a sloppy sled-team of dogs of all sizes—inserts change into the vending machine. Louise's interest is piqued. The dog-walker gruffly opens the door to the vending machine, but rather than removing a single newspaper he steals the entire supply, which he then uses to clean up dog poop from the sidewalk.

Louise, deflated, exasperated, finally turns to face Denny and Rach. "You can send him in," she says.

Brett the Banker goes in the office and Louise shuts the door, leaving Rach and Denny outside, attempting to eavesdrop on the conversation.

Rach is distressed. "When I agreed to move from Brooklyn I was promised an open work environment. Do you realize how severe my FOMO has become, living in Columbus, Ohio? Why are there bankers showing up in the middle of the day?"

"It shouldn't come as a surprise that the paper has been under-performing," Denny says, fanning his mustache hairs across his upper lip. "That's why Louise brought you on. You're the hip marketing guru."

"I guess that's no surprise considering our current readership demographic is boomers and older-than-boomers."

"Do you have your phone on you?"

"Always. What if one of my top five group chats messages? The struggle is real. Why?"

"You're going to need to call an ambulance."

Through the door, Denny and Rach hear Louise emit a loud gasp, followed by a thud as a body lands upon the floor.

When the EMTs arrive and roll Louise out of the building on a stretcher, they instruct Denny and Rach to call Louise's next of kin.

"Next of kin? That sounds serious," Rach says.

Denny peers off, as if studying an object on the horizon. "Speed Dog."

Meanwhile, at the annual Faerie Dragon & Latke Festival in nearby western Pennsylvania, Randy is wearing a karate gi and speaking Serbo-Croatian with a neighboring food stall operator while sipping a lemon shake-up. Speed Dog is prepping a blender of buffalo queso when all of a sudden an electric charge shakes the air and sends him upright, stiff as a board. He knows that something dramatic has happened.

Randy and Speed Dog quickly shutter their food stall and start driving Interstate 70 to Columbus. The Aerostar cuts a cool swath of quicksilver as it races down the highway.

At the hospital, Denny fills Speed Dog in. "Louise was employing her fake fainting technique—"

"Classic Louise," Speed Dog says, knowing the technique well.

"—but when she pretended to pass out, she hit her head. They ran tests and determined she suffered a mild concussion."

Randy puts his doctor hat on: "Mild Traumatic Brain Injury. Louise will need to limit both her physical and mental activities for the next week."

Rach is severely distressed. She's a millennial, so she wears it on her sleeve. "What about the paper, and Brett—the debt collector with the overactive hair gel and the calf tattoos? We literally do not have a week."

The crew stands in silence, digesting this information. What they need is a plan.

Punk Rock

BRUNCH

Chilaquiles—p. 37

Chilaquiles

CHILAQUILES

THE DISH: These chilaquiles make for either a solid brunch or dinner option, we're not ones to judge. For further blasphemy, drizzle this chilaquiles plate with hollandaise sauce (p. 47).

RED ENCHILADA SAUCE RECIPE

2 to 5 tostadas (fried corn tortillas)
2 cup vegetable broth
½ cup oil
½ cup crush tomato (or salsa)
½ cup flour*
3 tablespoons chili powder
2 tablespoons apple cider vinegar

1 tablespoon oregano
2 teaspoons onion powder
1 teaspoon smoked paprika
½ teaspoon cumin
½ teaspoon cinnamon
3 pieces garlic
½ or 1 dried chipotle pepper

CHEFFING INSTRUCTIONS

- In a blender, add spices, chipotle, vinegar, tomato, garlic, ½ cup broth.
- Add oil to a large pot. Once oil is warm, add flour.
- Pour blender contents into pot. Slowly add remaining broth.
- Simmer the tostadas until they absorb sauce.

ASSEMBLY

Form a bed of rice or quinoa, and top with pan-fried potatoes, chilaquiles, scramble (p. 44), buffalo queso (p. 10), and salsa (p. 28).

For a gluten-free version, use chickpea flour or similar.

FRENCH TOAST MONSTER

THE DISH: Look, you're basically making a monster of a breakfast sandwich out of french toast filled with compote, then covering with maple syrup. This recipe will delight kids or anyone craving something sweet for breakfast.

COMPOTE

2 pints berries
⅓ cup sugar
2 teaspoons lemon juice

FRENCH TOAST BATTER

15 ounces coconut milk
~1 cup plant milk, to desired consistency
1 cup sugar
½ cup flour
1 teaspoon cinnamon
vegan butter (p. 106) & bread

CHEFFING INSTRUCTIONS

- <u>Compote</u>: In pot, add berries, sugar, and lemon juice. Cover and heat, stirring occasionally until it resembles jam (roughly 20 to 30 minutes).
- <u>Batter</u>: In mixing bowl, add flour, cinnamon, sugar, and coconut milk. Whisk together ingredients, slowly adding plant milk until consistency is like papier-mâché—gooey, but not too thick.

ASSEMBLY

Heat vegan butter in a pan. Slice bread, dip in batter, and cook in pan. Once cooked, add warm compote to inside of french toast, like a sandwich. Drizzle with maple syrup.

PAIRING SUGGESTIONS

We listen to French electro-pop while brunch-cheffing. Can you tell?

French Toast Monster

Banh Mi Op La

BANH MI OP LA

THE DISH: This banh mi op la should be on your mood board right beside Rihanna's entrance to the Met Gala in 2018.

CHAR-SIU BARBECUE SAUCE RECIPE

1 cup crushed tomato
1/3 cup apple cider vinegar
1/4 cup sugar
2 tablespoons molasses
1 tablespoon white miso paste
2 teaspoons red chili flakes
2 teaspoons smoked paprika
2 teaspoons liquid smoke
1 teaspoon onion powder
2 pieces garlic

JACKFRUIT PORTION

48 ounces jackfruit
1 tablespoon oregano
1 tablespoon molasses
1 teaspoon onion powder

CHEFFING INSTRUCTIONS

• Blend all sauce ingredients to make char-siu barbecue sauce.
• Drain canned jackfruit, which should be quartered. Remove the harder core from the jackfruit with a knife.
• Add jackfruit to a large pot. Coat with 1 tablespoon oregano, 1 tablespoon molasses, 1 teaspoon onion powder. Cover jackfruit with char-siu barbecue sauce from blender and heat on high.
• As jackfruit simmers in sauce, use a potato masher to mash up the jackfruit so that it is no longer in quarters, but is stringy.

BANH MI OP LA, THE SAGA CONTINUES

WALNUT PATE RECIPE

¾ cup walnuts
¼ cup water
2 tablespoons nutritional yeast
1 tablespoon coconut oil
1 tablespoon lemon juice
1 tablespoon vegan Worcestershire
½ tablespoon white miso paste
1 teaspoon smoked paprika
½ teaspoon onion powder
1 piece garlic

JACKFRUIT

CHEFFING INSTRUCTIONS

• Add all ingredients to blender and pulverize.

ASSEMBLY

Smear walnut pate on bread.
Add sliced cucumbers, jalapeños, the char-siu jackfruit (p. 41),
and pickled vegetables such as carrots and daikon radish (p. 104).
Drizzle with warm hollandaise sauce (p. 47).
Top with fresh cilantro.

PAIRING SUGGESTIONS

Cambodian surf rock.
Slippers on a cold day.

Banh Mi Op La
with Walnut Pate

BUNNY CHOW

THE DISH: During the early days of covid, it became difficult to get certain items. Tofu, for one. So we took our old tofu scramble recipe and one-upped it by adding eggplant, red peppers, and garbanzo beans. When tofu became available again, we added it to the recipe to lighten it a bit.

SCRAMBLE RECIPE

½ eggplant
¼ red pepper
7.5 ounces coconut milk
14 ounces firm tofu
3 cups garbanzo beans
½ cup nutritional yeast
1 tablespoon lemon juice

1 tablespoon vegan Worcestershire
1 tablespoon parsley
1 tablespoon oregano
1½ teaspoon salt
1 teaspoon pepper
½ teaspoon curry

CHEFFING INSTRUCTIONS

- Peel skin off eggplant, cube and bake with red pepper until cooked.
- Add cooked eggplant, red pepper, coconut milk, and beans to blender.
- In mixing bowl, add tofu and spices; with cleans hands mash everything together. Add the contents of blender and stir.

ASSEMBLY

- Remove inside of bread to create a bread bowl.
- Heat scramble and hollandaise sauce (p. 47) in separate pans.
- Sauté sliced plantains in pan.
- Put scramble in bread bowl, top with hollandaise sauce and coconut bacon (p. 47). Stick the plantains up in bread bowl like bunny ears.

Bunny Chow

Breakfast Mollette

BREAKFAST MOLLETTE

THE DISH: Some people just want to eat with their hands. And that's cool, that's cool. A mollette—an open-faced sandwich—is a great way to eat with your hands while ensuring that you get sauce in your moustache.

COCONUT BACON

2 cups coconut flakes
1 tablespoon molasses
1 tablespoon liquid smoke
1 tablespoon vegetable oil
2 teaspoons smoked paprika
1 teaspoon onion powder
1 teaspoon pepper

HOLLANDAISE SAUCE RECIPE

15 ounces coconut milk
1 to 2 cups plant milk
½ cup vegetable oil
½ cup flour
2 tablespoons nutritional yeast
4 teaspoons lemon juice
1 teaspoon onion powder
1 teaspoon salt
½ teaspoon curry powder

CHEFFING INSTRUCTIONS

• Heat oil in pot. Once warm, add flour, spices, and coconut milk while stirring. Slowly add plant milk until sauce is smooth.
• Add oil to pot on low heat with coconut flakes and spices, stirring vigorously until the flakes absorb spices and oil.
• Warm scramble (p. 44) in pan.

ASSEMBLY

Slice hoagie bun in half and toast.
Top with scramble, hollandaise sauce, cheeze, and coconut bacon.

Chapter 2

The hospital discharged Aunt Louise to her nephew Speed Dog's care. After a single day of excessive pampering—which included Randy's Iron Goddess of Mercy oolong tea, transcendental meditation, and Speed Dog's legendary vegan cheffing (Speed Dog was not born a kitchen guy the same way that Bob Ross was not born a painter. What I'm talking about here are two things: Craftsmanship, and the Muse. He made chilaquiles for breakfast; falafels for lunch; almond pesto and mozzarella caprese for afternoon snacking; and oyster mushrooms with bechamel sauce for dinner)—Louise tried to sneak out of the house the next morning to go in to work.

"You need bed rest, Aunt Louise," Speed Dog said when he caught her.

"For goodness sakes, I fake fainted," she said in her defense. "Fake, as in not real."

Speed Dog scoffed. "But then you actually hit your head. Randy and I are going to stick around and help out until you're recovered."

"I am certified in barefoot shiatsu healing arts, kinetic healthcare, and CPR," chimed in Randy.

"I appreciate the sentiment, nephew, but you don't know the first thing about running a newspaper."

"Look," Speed Dog said, "you've been running that paper since the year Prince dropped *Purple Rain*. During that time, you've shouldered all the stress and anxiety that goes along with it. You've got a great team in Denny and Rach. Why not let them pick up some slack."

Louise mulled this silently. The fact that she was even considering the option felt like a minor victory. "I need some quiet," she finally said, conceding. "Take all these leftovers to Rach and Denny."

Later, in the *Gazette*'s breakroom, Rach and Denny stood side by side, curiously studying the Tupperware on the table.

"It's cool you have leftovers," Rach said, "but that doesn't mean your co-workers want your table scraps. Not everyone deserves a trophy."

"I do appreciate that they included the dietary information," Denny said, scanning the table for the ranch dressing.

"What are you allergic to?"

"No known allergies," Denny said, "just suspicions. Will you try it first and tell me if you taste any cardamom?"

In Louise's office, Randy is wearing a karate gi, doing the splits-between-chairs move of Jean-Claude Van Damme as seen in the blockbuster 1988 film *Bloodsport*. Speed Dog anxiously peers out of the window, eyeing the newspaper vending machine across the street, when Rach barges in. Randy opens one eye. Denny waits in the threshold and knocks politely, passively, obviously late.

"Denny and I have been talking," Rach said. There's more than a dollop of vegan farmhouse ranch dressing on his mustache. "We have an idea for a way to broaden newspaper readership and appeal outside of our core demographics of boomers and older-than-boomers."

"I'll admit to being a novice when it comes to marketing lingo," Speed Dog said, "but isn't that your job description?"

Denny politely smiles and nods his head. Rach ignores the remark. "Here's my pitch," she says. "Keep up." She forms her hands into a triangle and begins pacing the small office as she delivers her presentation. "*The Washington Post* calls the plant-based food industry 'the future of American cuisine,' saying '1 in 4' Americans eat more plant protein than before the pandemic. While the *BBC* says that 'more than half of Americans think it is important to eat sustainably.' Not to mention social media influencers like Alexandria Ocasio-Cortez—"

"Representative Ocasio-Cortez," Denny corrects her.

Rach is undeterred. "—citing a vegan diet as one of the best ways for individuals to personally combat climate change. And that doesn't count alternative lifestyles. I'm talking health-minded people, like those who may not identify as vegan but do yoga, or run half-marathons and put 13.1 bumper stickers on their Subaru."

"Cat people," Denny chimes in.

Rach shoots him a WTF look. "I have a cat," she says.

"I'm sure many own dogs as well," Denny says, defensively.

"Probably wouldn't say that they *own* pets if they're vegan," says Rach.

"I imagine they might say *pet partner* or *pet champion*. I'll look it up," Denny says.

Randy sees they've gotten off-track. "What are you suggesting?"

Rach leans forward on Louise's desk. "What I'm suggesting," she says, "is that the two of you write your own column in the *Gazette*."

"I'm glad you brought this up," Randy says. "I do have strong opinions about alternative hedonism and how it plays into capitalism and the current political moment."

"Okay, not that," Rach says. "The focus would be on food and vegan cooking, but it would also include your colorful personalities. There's lit-er-a-lly nothing like it."

Denny clears his throat, biting his tongue. Speed Dog finally takes a step back from the window. "Our back is against the wall, here, guys," he says. "Brett the Banker with the calf tattoos is about to shut us down, and the passionate, loyal advocate who built this paper into what it is over the past four decades is stuck at home with a mild traumatic brain injury. Your idea for how to save her livelihood is for two guys who have never written before to write a column for a central Ohio newspaper about vegan food?"

Rach and Denny appear to be hit by the gravity of the situation.

"This reminds me of the time a tropical storm swept our airboat to sea off the Gullah-Geechee coastline of South Carolina," Randy says. "We survived on algae and cinnamon fern."

51

"Columbus, Ohio, is the yoga studio of the Midwest," Rach says. "There's a 5k every weekend. I would say our community has a very strong passive interest in health issues such as a vegan diet. This is untapped market potential."

"Denny, you're the level head here," Speed Dog says, looking to him for affirmation. "What do you think?"

"I've been working with Louise for nearly those entire four decades," he says, "and in that time I've come to realize that while our community may not like yoga, we do like getting coffee after. While people may not like exercising or eating healthy, they do like to share recipes and health stories on Facebook." Everyone looks to one another waiting for the hammer to drop. "I believe we cannot continue with the status quo… It's worth a shot?"

PUB FOOD & SAMMYS

Walnut Chorizo Grilled Cheeze—p. 60

"Calamari" Fritti Sammy
When you're on the boardwalk you put it on a sammy, eat while walkin'.

BOUJEE BOARDWALK "CALAMARI" FRITTI SAMMY

THE DISH: This "calamari" is made using hearts of palm, which is a lovely, salty fish substitute. You can just as easily serve this as a "calamari" fritti appetizer.

"CALAMARI" FRITTI RECIPE

28 ounces hearts of palm
1 cup flour
~1 cup water
2 tablespoons lemon juice

1 tablespoon salt
1 tablespoon oregano
1 tablespoon vegan horseradish
2 teaspoon black pepper

CHEFFING INSTRUCTIONS

• Drain hearts of palm and rinse thoroughly.
• Slice hearts of palm in 1-inch pieces. To resemble calamari rings, remove the centers (centers can be saved for use in ceviche—p. 23).
• Add flour and spices to a mixing bowl. Whisk thoroughly, adding water till it resembles pancake batter.
• Add 1-inch-deep oil to pan and heat.
• Dip hearts of palm in flour mixture, then fry in oil.

ASSEMBLY

Add sliced tomatoes, fresh basil, pickled jalapeños (p. 104), slaw (p. 109), and some sriracha aioli (p. 107) racing stripes.

Farmhaus Breaded Tofu

FARMHAUS BREADED TOFU

THE DISH: What's more American than baseball and apple pie?
Breaded tofu, that's what.

RECIPE

16 ounces firm or extra firm tofu
2 cups flour
~2 cups vegan breadcrumbs
1/4 cup yellow mustard
3 teaspoons salt
2 teaspoons minced onion
1 teaspoon poultry seasoning
1 teaspoon dill

CHEFFING INSTRUCTIONS

• Add flour, mustard, and spices to a mixing bowl.
• Spread breadcrumbs out on a plate and set aside.
• Slowly add water while whisking until it resembles pancake batter.
• Slice tofu in half lengthwise. Then slice in ~1/4-inch pieces.
• Heat oil in pan at 1/2-inch depth.
• Dip tofu in mixture, then dip in breadcrumbs, then submerge in oil.

PAIRING SUGGESTIONS

Toss these bad boyz in char-siu barbecue sauce (p. 41).
Mark Wahlberg movies. Fall picnics on quilts.

BANANA PEEL BANH MI

THE DISH: Real talk: Banana peels are not only edible, they're packed with valuable nutrients like vitamin B12—enormously valuable for vegan diets—and dietary fiber. Farmers also use fewer pesticides on bananas since they have the protective peel. The texture and heartiness of cooked banana peels might be the closest we've found to resembling meat.

BANANA PEEL RECIPE

12 to 18 bananas, washed
2 cups vegetable broth
2 green peppers, sliced
5 pieces garlic, diced
2 tablespoons vegan Worcestershire

1 tablespoon oregano
1 teaspoon ginger powder
1 teaspoon cumin
1 teaspoon smoked paprika
½ teaspoon coriander
½ teaspoon onion powder

CHEFFING INSTRUCTIONS

- Remove top and bottom tip from banana peels. Remove bananas and set aside for other uses. Using a spoon, scrape the pulp from the inside of peel and discard. Using a fork, shred the peel.*
- Sauté diced garlic in a pan with oil. Add peels, spices, and broth. Cook on low heat in pan for 45 to 60 minutes, until peels are tender.

ASSEMBLY

- Add sliced cucumbers, walnut pate (p. 42), jalapeños, pickled carrots (p. 104), fresh cilantro, and lime aioli (p. 107) to the banana peels on a bun.

PAIRING SUGGESTIONS

The tears of your skeptics.

Food-grade gloves are recommended for this step.

Banana Peel Banh Mi

WALNUT CHORIZO GRILLED CHEEZE

THE DISH: We've done walnut chorizo before, but we improved it. How, you ask? Raisins, duh. (And chipotles.) Plus the coconut oil gives the chorizo an additional fattiness that really makes the mouth water. You can and should have this chorizo on tacos, with chilaquiles, or pretty much any food you're hoping to enjoy.

WALNUT CHORIZO RECIPE

1½ cups walnuts

1 cup garbanzo beans

½ cup coconut oil

½ cup raisins

2 tablespoons crushed tomato

1 tablespoon chili powder

1 tablespoon oregano

1 teaspoon apple cider vinegar

1 teaspoon onion powder

1 teaspoon sugar

1 teaspoon cinnamon

1 teaspoon cumin

2 pieces garlic, diced

1 chipotle pepper

CHEFFING INSTRUCTIONS

- Add everything except raisins and garlic to blender. Mix but don't pulverize, so that chunks of walnuts remain.
- Transfer contents of blender to mixing bowl and add raisins.
- In pan with light oil on medium heat, sauté garlic. Add walnut mixture, stir, and cover with lid. Cook chorizo until it begins to dry out and gets a nice cooked color (roughly 20 minutes).

ASSEMBLY

Cut a loaf of bread into thick slices and coat both sides with garlic butter (p. 106). Add walnut chorizo, sliced cheeze (p. 9), pimento cheeze (p. 6), pickled onions (p. 104), tomatoes, banana peppers, and toast it.

Walnut Chorizo Grilled Cheeze
Yes, pleaze.

"MEAT"BALL SUB

THE DISH: You can serve these "meat"balls over pasta, or in any other way that you can think of to devour "meat"balls. It just so happens that our fave way to devour them is in the pub, as a "meat"ball sub.

"MEAT"BALL RECIPE

1 eggplant, peeled, cubed
2 cups cooked lentils
~½ cup vegan breadcrumbs
½ cup vegetable protein (TVP)
½ cup hot water
1 tablespoon fennel seed

1 tablespoon oregano
1 tablespoon vegan Worcestershire
1 teaspoon cumin
1 teaspoon onion powder
2 pieces garlic

CHEFFING INSTRUCTIONS

- Cook peeled, cubed eggplant in a pan, drizzled with light oil.
- Add cooked eggplant to a blender with garlic and blend.
- In mixing bowl, add vegetable protein and hot water. Allow to thicken for ~10 minutes, then add lentils, spices, and blender contents. Stir and begin adding breadcrumbs until compact enough to form balls.
- Form the mixture into balls 1½ to 2 inches in diameter and place on cooking sheet.
- Bake in oven at 350°F for 15 minutes. Flip balls and bake for another 15 minutes.

PAIRING SUGGESTIONS

The wind in your hair while taking a ride on the Vengabus.

"Meat"Ball Sub in the Pub

Chapter 3

Randy is upside-down, doing a handstand while balanced against the wall. Speed Dog is seated before an empty desk in a nondescript office at the *Gazette*. On a wall is a dry-erase board, where Rach stands with a marker, hand on hip. She has written "Speed Dog and Randy's Food Column Mood Board" under which reads "Slaying vegan hunger demons," "throuple," and "Voyager 1 + Voyager 2."

"I'm just going to come out and say what we're all thinking," Randy says. "I don't know what to write about."

"I love vegan food and I love eating, but how does that amount to a newspaper column?" Speed Dog says.

Rach gasps. "It's not about eating and it's not about food. We're selling readers on a lifestyle, and you two are the brand."

Speed Dog makes a face like his head just exploded. "Now I'm more confused," he says.

"What you just said, Rach, ties more into my ideas on alternative hedonism than vegan cheffing," says Randy.

"Can you sit up so we can have a serious conversation?"

"I do my best thinking while in downward-facing tree."

"I'm grateful you guys are willing to stay and take a stab at writing this column," Rach says, exasperated, "but if you're not going to take it seriously then we won't get anywhere and may as well hand the keys over to Brett the Banker with the calf tattoos." Rach storms out of the room, slamming the door behind her.

"I thought millennials were supposed to be v chill," Randy says.

Speed Dog shakes his head and looks off into the distance, reflecting. "This reminds me of that time at Devil's Tower in Wyoming. Remember that?"

"I do. A good lesson in learning to go with the flow." Randy descends from the downward-facing tree and stands. "That young couple's VW van broke down and they were arguing about what to do."

"We were trying to make it to Sheridan for the annual Rodeo Festival."

"What were their names?" Randy asks.

"Jack and Diane."

"Not every white person's name is a John Mellencamp song."

Speed Dog waits.

Randy thinks about it. "Although in this case I believe you are correct," he says.

Just outside of Devil's Tower, Wyoming. The sun is a beast in the sky. A young twentysomething couple—Jack and Diane—are arguing beside a VW van that has broken down. Smoke steams from beneath the hood. The Aerostar drives by the VW, Speed Dog at the helm. After a short distance, Speed Dog and Randy exchange a look, and Speed Dog pulls a U-turn.

Unable to fix the bus, Speed Dog, Randy, Jack, and Diane search for a place to stay the night, but can only find a commercial campground outside Campstool Draw. There's a sorry-looking pool, a sorry-looking bandshell, a sorry-looking vending machine for food. Randy, Speed Dog, Jack, and Diane all exchange looks.

At a neighboring campsite, a mariachi band looks exhausted, as though the sorry state of the campground has sucked away their life-force. They are lounging around, shirts untucked; the sequins on their outfits do not glimmer. A hungry mariachi sits on a log near the woods. His stomach growls audibly so that everyone in the campground hears. Everyone immediately looks around, concerned.

In the dark of the woods behind the hungry mariachi, dozens of devilish red eyes alight: Hunger Demons. In the distance, a wolf howls ominously.

"What was that?" Jack asks.

"Hunger Demons," Diane replies. "I saw them once before, at a surprise 50th birthday party where not a single person remembered to bring food. Hunger Demons spare no one." She looks terrified.

Randy and Speed Dog lock eyes, deeply concerned. "We don't have much time," Speed Dog says.

Speed Dog and Randy rush to the Aerostar, where they quickly assemble a series of cooking supplies. The howling becomes more intense, as though the Hunger Demons are circling the campground.

A twig cracks in the woods. Jack, Diane, and the mariachi band have formed a tight huddle for safety.

Suddenly, a Hunger Demon leaps from the brush and violently drags the Hungry Mariachi into the darkness of the woods, leaving behind them a trail of blood.

Randy and Speed Dog are vegan cheffing as fast as they can. Sweat pours down their brows. "I don't think we have enough for everyone," Randy says. "What do we do?"

Speed Dog looks across the campground where he spots the sorry-looking vending machine. "We improvise," he says. Rifling through the Aerostar's cupholder, Speed Dog snatches a cup of change and looks to the vending machine: it's clear across the campground and far from the safety of the group. "Cover me!" he shouts.

Randy cracks a knuckle and unzips his fanny pack, removing a ninja star.

After looking side to side, Speed Dog bursts into a sprint with the cup of change. Randy is poised with the ninja star, prepared to throw. A single bead of sweat slowly rolls down his face: he doesn't wipe it.

Speed Dog makes it nearly halfway to the vending machine before a Hunger Demon emerges from the brush and violently charges toward him. The Hunger Demon is nearly upon Speed Dog when it is struck by a ninja star and drops to the ground. A cartoon bird circles its head. A handful of Hunger Demons take that as their cue, and rush Speed Dog from all directions.

Each Hunger Demon is met by one of Randy's ninja stars. Speed Dog completes his sprint to the vending machine and begins quickly inserting change. Bags of chips drop to the bottom slot and Speed Dog bear-hugs them to his chest.

A bit later, with the promise of a satisfying vegan meal on the horizon, the mood at the commercial campground has dramatically changed. The campground no longer looks sorry. At the cooking station, Randy and Speed Dog pass out food to everyone by spooning jackfruit "carnitas" into a bag of chips, which they top with jalapeños and grated vegan cheeze. The eyes of the Hunger Demons in the dark woods extinguish while the mariachis play their instruments with gusto.

"We fire-roasted jackfruit carnitas with quick-pickled jalapeños and made walking tacos," Randy says. "And the next day Jack and Diane taught us how to kitesurf at Keyhole Reservoir."

"That whole day was a mood," says Speed Dog. "Maybe we should write about that?"

Randy flicks his Kentucky Waterfall over his shoulder and shrugs. "Seems like as good an idea as any."

DINNER

OYSTER MUSHROOMS WITH BECHAMEL SAUCE

THE DISH: Oyster mushrooms pack a naturally nutritious punch, are rich with protein and low in calories, in addition to their lingering umami flavor. The combination of mushrooms and bechamel sauce is excellent over rice or on a buttery bread like a croissant.

RECIPE

3 to 4 cups oyster mushrooms
2 cups plant milk
¼ cup vegan cheeze
¼ cup coconut oil
¼ cup flour
2 tablespoons garlic butter (p. 106)
1 tablespoon oregano
1 teaspoon thyme
½ teaspoon onion powder
Salt + pepper to taste

CHEFFING INSTRUCTIONS

- <u>Mushrooms</u>: Clean mushrooms thoroughly. Heat garlic butter in pan, add oyster mushrooms, and sauté.
- <u>Sauce</u>: In a pot, heat coconut oil. Add flour and spices, then slowly add milk while whisking. Add cheeze and stir.

PAIRING SUGGESTIONS

A patio. A late-summer breeze.

**Oyster Mushrooms
with Bechamel Sauce**

She Is
Haunted

She Is Haunted

Paige Clark

Eggplant
Parmigiana

EGGPLANT PARMIGIANA

THE DISH: Eggplant parmigiana was an early gateway to a world of vegetarian dining. Eggplant remains a favorite cheffing ingredient to craft a meal around, and this parmigiana recipe will delight adults and kids alike.

BREADED EGGPLANT RECIPE

1 eggplant, washed
2 cups oil
2 cups vegan breadcrumbs
1½ cups flour
½ cup plant milk
1 tablespoon oregano
2 teaspoons salt

CHEFFING INSTRUCTIONS

• Remove ends of eggplant but keep the skin on. Slice across width in ¼-inch rings. Place slices on a rack with a towel beneath. Sprinkle with light salt, allowing the bitterness to release.
• In a mixing bowl, add flour and spices. Add milk, whisk, then add water and whisk until mixture resembles pancake batter.
• Pat the eggplant dry. Add breadcrumbs to plate and heat oil to high heat in a pan. Dip eggplant in the mixture, then in the breadcrumbs, then cook in the oil until golden brown.
• Serve over noodles tossed with marinara and drizzle with grated mozzarella cheeze (p. 9).

FALAFEL

THE DISH: Falafels are hearty and taste fresh. What's not to love?

RECIPE

8 ounces dry garbanzo beans (don't use canned beans)
⅓ cup onion, diced
1 tablespoon tahini
1 teaspoon cumin
1 teaspoon salt
1 teaspoon baking powder
1 bunch fresh dill
1 bunch fresh parsley
2 pieces garlic

CHEFFING INSTRUCTIONS

- Soak the dry beans for 20 to 24 hours.
- Add beans, spices, herbs, and onion to a blender and blend.
- Stir baking powder into mixture and let sit for an hour.
- Heat oil in pan at ½-inch depth.
- Form falafels into 2-inch diameter balls and fry in oil at high heat.

PAIRING SUGGESTIONS

Hummus (p. 25) and hot sauce (p. 105)!
Slice red cabbage super thin, toss it with light salt, and massage
until tender; then mix with fresh lemon balm from the garden.

Falafels

Kimchi & Fried Tofu

KIMCHI & FRIED TOFU

THE DISH: Fried food is an easy sell, and kimchi is such a flavorful addition for any dish. We recommend adding kimchi to tacos, sandwiches, or anything you want to give an extra spicy pop to.

KIMCHI RECIPE

1 large green cabbage
2 bunches of scallions (~10 scallions)
1 cup cilantro leaves
½ cup water
½ cup chili powder
2 tablespoons red miso paste
1 tablespoon sugar
Salt
8 pieces of garlic

CHEFFING INSTRUCTIONS

• Peel leaves of the cabbage. Tear into 2-inch chunks or slice into shreds like coleslaw (it's a person choice; we prefer shreds). Sprinkle cabbage with salt, roughly massage until it softens.
• Add garlic, scallion whites, spices, miso, and water to blender.
• Pour mixture over cabbage, roughly rub together.
• Add cilantro and scallion greens. Push down cabbage until submerged in juices. Sit out for 24 hours to ferment.

ASSEMBLY

Serve with farmhaus breaded tofu (p. 57) on bed of quinoa or rice.

Curry Enchiladas

CURRY ENCHILADAS

THE DISH: Enchiladas are a dinner staple, but sometimes it's fun to mix up the sauce. The balance of fresh basil, lime, jalapeños, and yellow curry is delightful. Stacked as an enchilada, it's bewitching.

15 ounces coconut milk
3 to 4 cups quinoa or rice, cooked
2 cups lentils, cooked
¾ cup vegetable broth
¼ cup fresh basil, chopped
1½ tablespoons lime juice
6 tablespoons oil

YELLOW CURRY RECIPE

6 tablespoons chickpea flour
1 to 2 jalapeños, diced
1½ tablespoon yellow curry powder
½ teaspoon salt
½ teaspoon onion powder
½ teaspoon sugar
3 pieces roasted garlic

CHEFFING INSTRUCTIONS

- Blend coconut milk, spices, lime juice, garlic, and vegetable broth.
- Heat oil in pot. Add flour. Slowly add contents from blender while whisking until consistency is a hearty, thick sauce.
- In a pan with light oil, sauté jalapeños and cooked lentils. Combine with quinoa or rice and fresh basil in a mixing bowl.
- Heat corn tortillas in a pan.
- Layer tortillas with bowl contents and smother with curry sauce.

PAIRING SUGGESTIONS

Anyone you want to impress with your cheffing prowess. Hot sauce. Instead of lentils, substitute sautéed mushrooms, tofu, or eggplant.

PIZZA

THE DISH: Look, this is the most important recipe in the book, not gonna lie. We can teach you how to chef banana peels and all kinds of wild and exciting things, but pizza night is every Friday!

PIZZA DOUGH RECIPE

5 cups flour
2¼ cup super hot water
¼ cup oil
1 tablespoon fast-rise baking yeast
1 tablespoon flax seed
1 tablespoon oregano
1 teaspoon salt
1 teaspoon curry

CHEFFING INSTRUCTIONS

- Add flour and dry ingredients to mixing bowl, then oil, and the hot water last.
- Mix ingredients by spoon, and then finish by hand. Add flour as needed while continuing to knead by hand. (You want the dough to be springy; you gotta give it love; pizza dough is all about feel.)
- Let dough sit for at least 2 hours. Then heat oven to 500°F; toss in pinches of flour so not sticky, and continue to knead dough.
- Make the dough in to 2 pizza crusts, curling up the edges.
- Cover the dough with marinara sauce and shredded mozzarella cheeze (p. 9), and favorite toppings.
- Bake at 500°F for 15 to 20 minutes, or until crust is crunchy.

Chapter 4

The parking lot at Whole Foods in the suburbs mid-afternoon on a week day is like a James Taylor song. V chill. V sleepy. Immediately next to the entryway is a *Mid-Ohio Weekly Gazette* newspaper vending machine.

Inside the market, an informal, extracurricular Parent Teacher Organization meeting, comprised only of parents, is in progress. Karen is sitting at a banquet table beside Karen-Katherine (both of whom are eternally 39) and a gaggle of other cookie-cutter suburban women. We spy Blue Lives Matter pins, blond hair in bobs, spray tans, single-color polo shirts, snug slacks, and jeans with fashionable rips. In the Whole Foods food court, the women stab at salads and nibble lukewarm trofie pasta from the hot bar. In the center of the table rests a copy of the *Mid-Ohio Weekly Gazette*, which each of the women appears to have passive-aggressively spilled food on.

"What I don't understand," Karen says, "is how the lamestream media gets away with publishing drivel like this. There's no warning or disclaimer. What if one of our kids just picked up the paper and started reading an article about vegan foods and alternative lifestyles." Karen stabs an accusative nail-polished finger on Speed Dog and Randy's profile pictures on the cover of the *Gazette*.

"My kids' tutor hasn't taught them to read yet," Karen-Katherine chimes in, "and I still find that thought very triggering."

"O-M-G," Karen says, "I shudder to think how it could possibly be any more triggering. That thought is the most triggering."

All the women at the table mumble their agreement. Some visibly shudder.

"A line has been crossed," Karen continues. "This subversive, radical, far left agenda needs to be stopped."

A Black teenager named Dwayne is tidying up the food court and overhears the PTO meeting. "What you're talking about reminds me of something that Noam Chomsky said," Dwayne says. He pinches his face in thought while Karen, Karen-Katherine, and all the other women look aghast at having their conversation interrupted. They can't speak; they're speech-less. "Or maybe it was Peter Singer?" Dwayne continues. "Doesn't matter, some old dude. But he said—and I'm paraphrasing here—'Either you repeat the same conventional doctrines everybody is saying, or else you say something true, and it will sound like it's from freaking Neptune.'"

It's so quiet in the Whole Foods food court and the greater Whole Foods marketplace that you could hear a pin drop. In that moment, a literal pin drops. Karen looks like she is choking on a bone. Karen-Katherine anxiously fishes inside her purse and eventually finds an inhaler, which she removes and takes an emergency gulp of.

"Do you see how that applies to what you're discussing?" Dwayne asks. "These guys wrote a story about kitesurfing on a lake in Wyoming and shared a recipe for jackfruit carnitas—which, side note, I tried out and it's pretty dope. So what. Who cares? What's it got to do with you?"

The women take a massive synchronized gulp.

A handful of Dwayne's team members have sided with him in the food court.

"What's it got to do with us?!" Karen asks.

"What's it got to do with us?!" Karen-Katherine echoes.

"It's not hurting you in any way," Dwayne says. "A vegan diet is just a healthier way of eating that's better for the planet."

"I feel sorry for you," Karen says, "because there is clearly a problem with how you were raised. Maybe your father wasn't at home."

"My dad raised me. Two dads, actually."

"Two dads?" Karen-Katherine asks, hand on chest, slumped back in her chair.

"They're married," Dwayne says, matter-of-factly.

"I quite literally have never in my entire life been this disrespected," Karen says. "This treatment is appalling, and makes me equally embarrassed for the entire Whole Foods brand and for Jeff Bezos. What would Jeff Bezos think of this abhorrent behavior?"

"I think all Jeff Bezos cares about is you paying $15 for microwaved pasta," Dwayne says.

"I am soooo opposed to raising the minimum wage," Karen says.

"Hashtag shocker. White privilege is real."

Karen lifts her tray of food from the table. Karen-Katherine follows suit, as do all the women. Karen locks eyes with Dwayne and then spills her tray full of uneaten food all over the cafeteria floor. A Whole Foods team member uncaps their Hydro Flask and chucks the contents—including damp mate tea leaves—all over the PTO. Hell breaks loose. Punk music probably plays. It's a good old fashioned food fight. But instead of yelling "food fight," one of Dwayne's team members shouts, "Class war!"

MUNCHIES

Pambazo de Chilaquiles—p. 93

Caprese Sandwich

CAPRESE SANDWICH

THE DISH: This sandwich is so European I can't even go there. It's perfect for a light lunch or mid-afternoon snack after smashing some hardcore volleys at the racquet club.

ASSEMBLY

- Cut thick slices of tomatoes and mozzarella cheeze (p. 9).
- Toast a bun, and smear with creamy almond pesto (p. 17).
- Layer the tomatoes and sliced mozzarella in a super classy way on the bun. Smear the top of the bun with a generous serving of almond pesto.

PAIRING SUGGESTIONS

Sweaters you don't actually wear but casually tie over your shoulders while playing tennis or pickleball. The crinkly sound when you turn the page of a newspaper. Noon tea.

FARMHAUS BREADED TOFU TORTUGA

THE DISH: This one goes out to the punk boys on Friday afternoons.

ASSEMBLY

• Slather farmhaus breaded tofu (p. 57) in hot sauce (p. 105) and bake.

• In a large flour tortilla, add shredded cheeze (p. 9), banana peppers, pickled onions (p. 104), coconut bacon (p. 47), and extra love.

• Roll up tortilla and heat in oven till it gets crispy and Tortuga-ized.

PAIRING SUGGESTIONS

Hamms. A stick-and-poke tattoo.

TORTUGA

JALAPEÑO POPPER BAGEL

THE DISH: Breaded Eggplant + Cream Cheeze + Pickled Jalapeños legit tastes exactly like a jalapeño popper pretty much. Now put it on a bagel.

ASSEMBLY

- Slice and toast your favorite type of bagel.
- Heat breaded eggplant (p. 73) in a pan on light heat.
- Add pickled jalapeños (p. 104) and an unhealthy amount of cream cheeze (p. 5) to your bagel.

PAIRING SUGGESTIONS

Crush this in your car when no one's looking.

Pambazo de Chilaquiles
with a side of more potatoes.

PAMBAZO DE CHILAQUILES

THE DISH: Look, sometimes you just don't want a protein shake after "Strength Cardio and Core" class. Is that okay with you Coach Catie? (Rhetorical question, Coach.)

ASSEMBLY

- A pambazo is a Mexico City-style "wet" sandwich. Dip the outside of a hoagie bun in hot sauce (p. 105) and toast in a warm pan on both sides. You still want it damp; it's not called a Mexico City-style "dry" sandwich, after all.
- Make chilaquiles by cooking tostadas in red enchilada sauce. (See the full recipe on p. 37)
- Put some potatoes on there, some buffalo queso (p. 10), and hollandaise sauce (p. 47). Hit the gym (extra hard) the next day.

Banana Peel Cheezesteak

BANANA PEEL CHEEZESTEAK
A.K.A. THE BILLY CHEEZESTEAK

THE DISH: This sandwich is Philly meets Ponce, a Caribbean twist on the classic from the City of Brotherly Love.

ASSEMBLY

- In a pan with coconut oil, warm banana peel shreds (p. 58) with sliced peppers.
- Swipe a generous serving of pimento cheeze spread (p. 6) on a toasted bun.
- Add shredded cabbage, tomato, pickled onions (p. 104), and aioli (p. 107).

PAIRING SUGGESTIONS

A fine American lager with hot-sauce-salted rim.
Watching the Birds game on the TV with all your close Bubs.
Before or after a good cry from watching *Rocky IV*.

Fully-Loaded

DESSERTS

**Carrot Cake
Bars—p. 100**

Lemon-Blueberry Cupcakes

LEMON-BLUEBERRY CUPCAKES

THE DISH: These cupcakes taste like summer without being overwhelming. Great for sharing, they make a perfect addition to any picnic.

MUFFIN RECIPE

2 cups flour
1 cup sugar
1 cup almond milk
1 cup blueberries
⅓ cup oil

2 tablespoons lemon juice
1 tablespoon apple cider vinegar
2 teaspoons baking powder
1 pinch salt
zest of 1 lemon

CHEFFING INSTRUCTIONS

• Pre-heat oven to 350°F.
• In liquid measuring cup, add almond milk and vinegar. Let curdle.
• Add dry ingredients to mixing bowl and stir. Add wet ingredients and stir. Add blueberries last, stirring gently.
• Disperse mixture in 12-cup muffin pan after spraying.
• Bake 30 minutes, or until able to insert toothpick and remove.

PAIRING SUGGESTIONS

Top with frosting (p. 100) to make the king of cupcakes.

CARROT CAKE BARS

THE DISH: These carrot cake bars are chewy and delicious, without being overly sweet, which allows the raisins to really pop.

FROSTING RECIPE

2 cups powdered sugar
⅔ cup oil
⅓ cup plant milk

CHEFFING INSTRUCTIONS

- <u>Carrot Cake Bars</u>: Pre-heat oven to 350°F.
- In liquid measuring cup, add almond milk and vinegar. Let curdle.
- Add dry ingredients to mixing bowl. Add carrots, walnuts, raisins, and then the wet ingredients.

CARROT CAKE BAR RECIPE

2 cups flour
2½ cups carrots, coarsely grated
1 cup sugar
½ cup walnut pieces
¾ cup almond milk
½ cup raisins
¼ cup oil
1 tablespoon apple cider vinegar
2½ teaspoon cinnamon powder
2½ teaspoon baking powder
½ teaspoon nutmeg
½ teaspoon ginger powder

- Transfer mixture to a 6-inch by 9-inch pan and bake for ~35 minutes or until able to insert a toothpick to center and remove.
- <u>Frosting</u>: In mixing bowl, add ingredients and mix with a hand mixer at a high speed. Refrigerate while allowing carrot cake bars to cool before topping with frosting.

PAIRING SUGGESTIONS

Thanksgiving. John Cusack movies.

Carrot Cake Bars

LIFE-HACKS

Falafel in a Wrap—p. 74

QUICK-PICKLED VEGGIES

THE DISH: A simple pickled vegetable garnish can go a long way in terms of making dishes look classy AF. You can add pickled onions, jalapeños, and carrots to salads, tacos, burgers, or whatever, but you've gotta eat with your pinkies up.

INGREDIENTS
~2 cups hot water
1 cup apple cider vinegar

2 tablespoons sugar
3 teaspoons salt
2 onions, jalapeños, or carrots

CHEFFING INSTRUCTIONS
- Cut vegetable into thin slices.
- In a container, add vegetable slices, then top with sugar, salt, and vinegar. Top with hot water until everything is completely submerged.
- Allow to cool for an hour before refrigerating.

SUGGESTIONS
You can quick-pickle any vegetables this way. It's fast and easy, and you can refrigerate them and store the pickled veggies for later.

← PICKLED ONIONS ON EVERYTHING →

HOT SAUCE

THE DISH: Once you make your own hot sauce, you'll never go back to store-bought swill. Hot sauce is super easy to make and really only requires two key components: xanthan gum (for consistency, so it's not a watery mess), and a decent blender.

HOT SAUCE BASE

~2 cups of hot peppers,
of your choosing
1 cup water
½ cup white vinegar
2 teaspoons celery salt
1 teaspoon sugar
¼ teaspoon xanthan gum (stirred with
2 tablespoons water, and allowed to sit)

CHEFFING TIPS

• We roast the peppers so they acquire a slightly smoky, charred taste.
  • On top of the base, you can get creative and add things like lime juice, tequila, smoked paprika, lime zest, cilantro, canned chipotles, or whatever else you feel would make the sauce diabolical.
• Blend everything together, completely pulverizing it. Then add the xanthan gum/water mixture and pulverize a second time. Allow hot sauce to sit for an hour before refrigerating. With the vinegar, the hot sauce will last for up to a month.

GARLIC BUTTER

THE DISH: Garlic butter on everything. That's the truth.

GARLIC BUTTER RECIPE

1 cup coconut oil
⅓ cup unsweetened plant milk
2 tablespoon vegetable oil
1½ teaspoons nutritional yeast
1 teaspoon dill
½ teaspoon salt
2 pieces garlic

CHEFFING INSTRUCTIONS

- Throw everything in a blender.
- Add more salt, to taste.
- Refrigerate, add to pretty much everything, and use for cooking.

MAYONNAISE (OR AIOLI, IF YOU'RE FANCY)

THE DISH: Figuring out how to make our own mayonnaise from scratch using aquafaba was a life-saver. Vegan mayo is pretty pricey at stores, and we use this creamy mayo as a base for everything from our farmhouse ranch dressing, to tartar sauce, remoulade, and on and on.

INGREDIENTS

3 cups oil

~1¼ cups tapioca flour

1 cup aquafaba

3 tablespoons lemon juice

1 tablespoon apple cider vinegar

1 teaspoon sugar, salt, pepper

2 teaspoons dill

2 teaspoons onion powder

5 to 7 pieces garlic

CHEFFING INSTRUCTIONS

Add aquafaba, lemon juice, sugar, salt, pepper, tapioca flour, and oil to a blender and pulverize until resembling a creamy mayonnaise. Add additional tapioca flour or aquafaba until it achieves desired consistency.

PAIRING SUGGESTIONS

Mix with sriracha for sriracha aioli.

Add something like roasted red peppers to impress bougie friends. The only thing holding you back is your imagination.

HOW TO PROPERLY LAYER A TACO

THE DISH: There's no recipe here. This is more of a lesson culled from life as to how to organize a taco the proper way. This is 30+ years of learned taco-eating experience. It's not dissimilar from acknowledging that there is a correct way to assemble a sandwich: bottom bun—patty—cheeze—fixin's.

Here is the life-hack for tacos: put a cheeze spread as the first layer of the taco, then add the base like seasoned "beef," or carnitas, or walnut chorizo, or whatnot. The spread acts as a glue and keeps the base from sliding off the tortilla.

HOW TO LAYER A TACO:

1. TORTILLA

2. CHEEZE SPREAD

3. FIXINS

4. SLAW, SALSA, AIOLI

SLAW

THE DISH: It's our adamant belief that you should add slaw to everything: tacos, burgers, salads, etc. Generally speaking, you can toss any kind of vegetables together for slaw, even broccoli and cauliflower, and toss with some light salt, sugar, vinegar, and citrus juice.

INGREDIENTS

2 tablespoons lime juice

1 tablespoon vinegar

1 teaspoon salt

1 teaspoon sugar

¼ cabbage

1 carrot, peeled

½ cup fresh cilantro, diced

½ cucumber, sliced length-wise, seeded

CHEFFING INSTRUCTIONS

• Thinly slice cabbage and grate carrots.

• Once the cucumber has been seeded, slice into thin quarter-moons.

• Add cabbage to a mixing bowl with salt and knead by hand. Then add remaining vegetables, cilantro, sugar, lime juice, and vinegar, and stir together thoroughly.

← SLAW ON EVERYTHING →

AQUAFABA

Aquafaba—literally "bean water"—is simply the liquid that beans have been cooked in, and it can be sourced from any bean. The easiest way to have it on hand is to open a can of ready-to-eat beans, pour the liquid portion into a lidded container, and keep it in the fridge.

White bean aquafaba is commonly used in recipes because of its neutral flavor, and what we suggest for the recipes in this book. Consider trying garbanzo, cannellini, great northern, or lima.

STOCKING THE PANTRY

If these (perhaps) less common items aren't already on your shelves at home, we suggest keeping them stocked in order to make vegan cheffing easy peasy.

- Apple cider vinegar (with "the mother")
- Bean cans for easy aquafaba (white beans)
- Breadcrumbs (containing no dairy)
- Cashews
- Coconut flakes
- Coconut milk cans
- Coconut oil
- Horseradish (containing no dairy)
- Kappa carrageenan
- Liquid smoke
- Milk from plants (soy, oat, nut)
- Miso paste (red and white)
- Nutritional yeast
- Tapioca flour
- Textured vegetable protein (TVP)
- Tofu
- Worcestershire sauce (containing no fish)
- Xanthan gum

Chapter 5

Across the heartland, from the yoga studios to the arts district's sports bars, from the unattractive brown water of the Scioto River to the hipster coffeeshops, Randy and Speed Dog's vegan food column is the talk of the town.

Outside the offices of the *Mid-Ohio Weekly Gazette* on the city's South End, Karen, Karen-Katherine, and the rest of the parents from the PTO are picketing the newspaper office. They hold signs that say "I want to see a manager!" and "Defund Public Healthcare!"

Opposite them is a diverse collection of opposition picketers, who tout signs declaring slogans like "Raise the Minimum Wage!" and "Black Lives Matter."

Neither gathering is enormous—this is the yoga studio of the Midwest, after all—but it is substantial enough that passing drivers slow their vehicles to check out what's going on. And whenever a passing car shouts a honk of support, both sides emit a victorious cheer assuming it's for their cause, while angrily glaring down the opposition.

From the window of the *Gazette*'s office, Rach and Denny study the crowds outside, intrigued. Speed Dog and Randy have joined them. They all appear concerned. Except Rach.

"I'll be the first to admit," Denny says, "that I dramatically underestimated the impact that Speed Dog and Randy's column would have."

"We were thirsty," Rach says excitedly, "and we made it purple rain!"

Shaking his head, visibly troubled, Speed Dog paces the room. "We should have listened to Denny, not to the marketing guru."

"Why would you think that?" Rach asks. "I'm a millennial, I have ideas. And opinions. And I won't apologize."

"There's a template," Speed Dog says. "We changed something that Louise has been laboring over since the year Prince dropped *Purple Rain*."

Echoing the voices in Speed Dog's head, the chorus of chants outside grows in volume, becoming audibly more rowdy.

"What's Aunt Louise going to say?" Speed Dog asks the room.

"If I had to make an informed guess," Denny says, "it would be that newspapers don't make news; they report news."

"Would you stop already being the voice of reason?" Rach says. "Think about it this way: we might be ushering in a new era, the dawn of 'engaged journalism.'"

Suddenly, as if on cue, Louise appears in the threshold of the office, wearing a power pantsuit. "Someone wanna tell me why the Upper Arlington Parent Teacher Organization is outside my building, eating steak tartare and drinking whole milk?"

Stay tuned for what happens next time!

Index

CHEEZES

DESSERTS

DRESSING & SAUCES & DIPS

SIDES & SOUPS

VEGGIE-BASED MEAT SUBSTITUTES

Recipes in Order of Appearance

ERIC OBENAUF is the Editorial Director of Two Dollar Radio, a press he founded with his wife, Eliza. Eric was included in *Publishers Weekly*'s "50 Under 40" list, spotlighting 50 individuals working in publishing under age 40 worth watching, and was one of five (5) finalists in the magazine's 2016 "Star Watch" awards.

At Two Dollar Radio Headquarters, Eric stocks the books and chefs it up in the kitchen. He enjoys camping, hiking, reading outside with a beer or two like a gentleman, and dad jokes. He is the author of the *Two Dollar Radio Guide to Vegan Cooking* series.

Two Dollar Radio acknowledges that this land where we live and work, commonly known as "Columbus, Ohio," is the contemporary territory of the Shawnee, Miami, Hopewell, and other Indigenous Nations,* which comprised some of the roughly 80,000 Indigenous people forcibly displaced from their ancestral homelands east of the Mississippi River** through the Indian Removal Act of 1830. We would like to pay our respects as well as honor the culture, heritage, and resiliency of these and other Indigenous nations with strong ancestral ties to these lands, as well as individuals from Indigenous backgrounds in our community who continue to call central Ohio home.

*https://native-land.ca/
**https://estoo-nsn.gov/educators-guide/movement/
***https://history.state.gov/milestones/1830-1860/indian-treaties
****https://nativegov.org/a-guide-to-indigenous-land-acknowledgment/

Two Dollar Radio Guide to Vegan Cooking: The Pink Edition is two things at once—a pra
guide to vegan cheffing, and a playful epic of the stories behind the recipes.

In this Pink Edition of the celebrated *Guide to Vegan Cooking* series, the saga cont
as executive chefs Jean-Claude van Randy and Speed Dog (with assists from
Obenauf) share comfort food recipes with an international flourish, such as **B
Chow**—a blasphemous bread bowl favored by South African surfers; **Chilaqui**
a Mexican breakfast dish, and finally something the *rockeros* and the *metaleros* can agre
and a **Banana Peel Banh Mi**—a riff on the classic Vietnamese sandwich using–
guessed it, banana peels! Rest assured, Chef Randy's Sheboygan roots run deep, as
is a dedicated section on vegan **"Cheezes,"** as well as debaucherous Midwestern st
like **Pimento Cheeze**, **French Toast Sandwiches**, and **Pizza**. Vegan Hunger Der
do not sleep. Thankfully Randy and Speed Dog are laced up and ready for battle.

This *Guide to Vegan Cooking* is for you if:
· You're looking for satisfying comfort food;
· You're interested in a vegan diet but are having trouble giving up cheese;
· You're searching for accessible vegan recipes that don't require
  hard-to-find ingredients you can't pronounce;
· You crave ADVENTURE.

$16.99
ISBN 978-1-953387-22-6
51699>

Trade Paperback Original
VEGAN COOKBOOK/STORIES

FSC
MIX
Paper from
responsible sources
FSC® C103567
www.fsc.org

9 781953 387226

Two Dollar Ra
Books too loud to Igi